HEA
COMPLEX PTSD

7 Practical Strategies to Heal Your Inner Child and Recover From Post-Traumatic Stress Disorder

(A Re-Parenting Map to Thriving and Surviving)

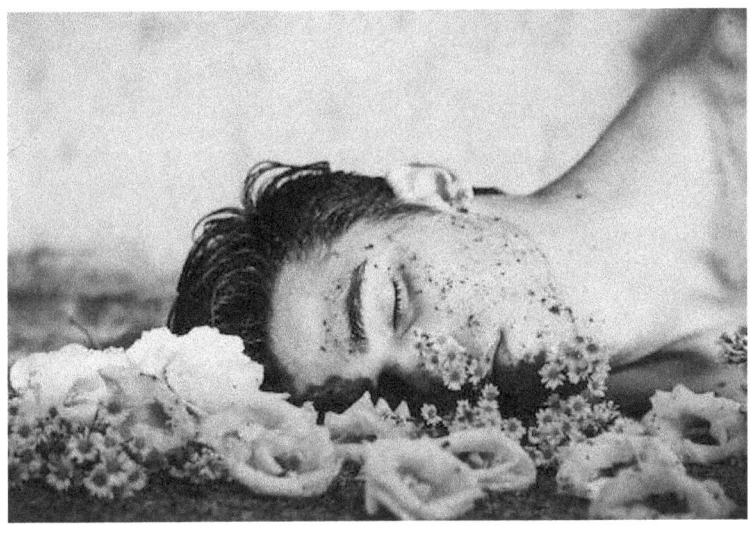

DR. KADEN WINTON

3 | HEALING COMPLEX PTSD

Dedication

To Those Who Carry the Weight of the Past,

This book is dedicated to you— the brave souls who have faced the unimaginable, who have endured the depths of pain and emerged with the strength to heal. It is for the child within you, whose innocence was stolen but whose spirit remains resilient.

To the ones who refuse to let their past define them, who search for hope amidst the shadows, we honor your unwavering courage and perseverance. Your journey of healing is an inspiration to us all.

May the pages of **"Healing Complex PTSD"** be a guiding light, a sanctuary of understanding, and a roadmap to reclaiming your life. As you immerse yourself in these words, know that you are seen, heard, and deeply cherished.

Through every tear shed and every breakthrough celebrated, may you find solace, strength, and the unwavering belief that healing is possible. You are not alone, dear reader. We walk beside you, offering our support, compassion, and the *promise that together, we can create a future filled with love, resilience, and limitless possibilities.*

With heartfelt dedication,

Dr. Kaden Winton and the Healing Complex PTSD Team

FREE EMAIL CONSULTATION

Dear Reader,

Thank you for choosing to embark on the healing journey with our book, *"Healing Complex PTSD"* Your support means the world to us, and we are deeply grateful for your trust.

As a token of our appreciation, we would like to offer you a unique opportunity. We are delighted to provide a complimentary email consultation where you`` can address any questions or challenges you may encounter while implementing the principles shared in our book.

Simply send me an email at wintonconsults@gmail.com and within 24 hours, you will receive a personalized response from me.

Please note that this free consultation offer is exclusively available to individuals who have purchased our book.

Once again, we extend our heartfelt thanks for your support, and we look forward to assisting you on your healing journey.

7 | HEALING COMPLEX PTSD

Table of Contents

Dedication 4

FREE EMAIL CONSULTATION 6

Introduction 13

Chapter One 19

    Understanding Complex PTSD in Childhood: Unraveling the Hidden Impact of Trauma 19

    Defining Complex PTSD in Childhood 19

    Recognizing Symptoms and Signs 20

    The Importance of Early Intervention and Support 22

Chapter Two 23

    Unveiling the Inner Child: Nurturing Healing and Reconnection 23

    Discovering the Concept of the Inner Child 23

    Understanding the Impact of Childhood Trauma on the Inner Child 24

    Recognizing the Presence and Needs of Your Inner Child 24

    Nurturing and Reconnecting with Your Inner Child 25

Chapter Three 27

    Building a Foundation of Safety and Trust 27

    Creating a Safe Environment for Healing 27

    Establishing Trust in Oneself and Others 28

    Healing Attachment Wounds and Building Healthy Relationships 28

Cultivating Self-Compassion and Self-Care Practices 29

Chapter Four 30

   Strategy 1: Reconnecting With the Inner Child 30

   Recognizing the Importance of Reconnecting with Your Inner Child 30

   Practical Techniques to Establish a Connection and Build Trust 31

   Rebuilding a Sense of Safety and Security for Your Inner Child 32

Chapter Five 35

   Strategy 2: Healing Traumatic Memories - Liberating the Past for a Brighter Future 35

   Understanding How Traumatic Memories are Stored and Triggered 35

   Processing and Integrating Traumatic Memories 36

   Utilizing Evidence-Based Therapeutic Techniques for Trauma Resolution 38

   Emotional and Physical Trauma Release from the Body 40

Chapter Six 42

   Strategy 3: Re-parenting the Inner Child - Nurturing the Wounded Self with Love and Compassion 42

   Becoming the Loving and Nurturing Parent Your Inner Child Needs 42

   Identifying and Challenging Negative Beliefs and Self-Talk .. 44

   Applying Re-parenting Techniques to Provide Comfort, Validation, and Support 45

Fostering Resilience and Self-Esteem in Your Inner Child 47

Chapter Seven 49

Strategy 4: Emotional Regulation and Self-Soothing - Nurturing Inner Calm and Well-Being 49

Developing Emotional Regulation Skills 49

Learning Effective Coping Mechanisms for Emotional Distress 50

Practicing Mindfulness and Grounding Techniques 52

Cultivating Self-Soothing Strategies for Emotional Well-Being 53

Chapter Eight 55

Strategy 5: Rebuilding Trust and Relationships - Nurturing Connections for Healing and Growth 55

Understanding the Impact of Trauma on Trust 55

Rebuilding Trust in Oneself and Others 57

Nurturing Healthy and Supportive Relationships 58

Establishing Boundaries and Communication Skills 59

Chapter Nine 61

Strategy 6: Empowering the Inner Child - Unleashing Strength, Growth, and Resilience 61

Encouraging Empowerment and Self-Advocacy 61

Cultivating Strengths and Talents 62

Setting Goals and Embracing Personal Growth 63

Fostering Resilience and Embracing Positive Change 65

Chapter Ten 67

Strategy 7: Integration and Continued Healing - Embracing Wholeness and Celebrating Growth 67

Integrating the Healed Aspects of the Inner Child with the Present Self 67

Forgiving and Letting Go of the Past 69

Sustaining Long-Term Recovery and Growth 70

Celebrating the Resilience and Growth of Your Inner Child .. 71

Bonus 73

   Self-Assessment Exercises 73

Bonus Two 85

   Positive Affirmations 85

Conclusion 87

Appreciation 90

Picture Links 92

Introduction

When I was just five years old, and my sister was four, we woke up in a hospital surrounded by blinding lights and sterile walls. Confusion clouded my young mind as a nurse with curly blonde hair and vibrant red lipstick attended to me. Strapped down on a stretcher, I struggled to recall what had happened. The memory of a tube down my throat still haunts me, evoking an intense aversion to gagging or throwing up. Despite my fear, I desperately wanted to bring a smile to the nurse's face. With each shot in my arm, I feigned unconsciousness, opening my eyes and letting out muffled laughter, coaxing a smile from her weary face.

But my father's sporadic appearances shattered the fleeting joy. Fear radiated from him, leaving me puzzled. It was only later, when I was older that I discovered the horrifying truth. Our mother had attempted to overdose us on her pills. The realization struck like a thunderbolt, leaving my sister and me scarred by the gravity of her actions. As the years passed, I eventually learned that it wasn't a psychotic break that drove her to such a heinous act. It was her anger towards my father's drinking, and she sought retribution by endangering our lives.

The impact of that traumatic event reverberated throughout our lives, casting a shadow over our sense of safety and trust. We carried the weight of those memories, grappling with the lasting effects of our mother's actions. But amidst the darkness, a beacon of hope emerged.

It was during our darkest moments that we discovered a book, a lifeline that offered guidance and healing. "Healing Complex PTSD Child: 7 Practical Strategies to Heal Your Inner Child and Recover from Post-Traumatic Stress Disorder (A re-parenting Map)" became our roadmap to recovery. With trepidation and determination, we delved into its pages, seeking solace and understanding.

Chapter by chapter, we embarked on a transformative journey. We learned to embrace our inner child, rebuild a foundation of safety and trust, and heal the wounds inflicted upon us. Through the strategies outlined in the book, we discovered the power of reconnecting with ourselves and nurturing broken parts. We uncovered the strength to face our traumatic memories head-on, finding ways to process and release the pain that had held us captive.

With each turn of the page, we embraced the art of re-parenting ourselves, offering the love, validation, and support we had longed for. We honed our emotional regulation skills, practicing self-care and soothing techniques to navigate the storms within us. We rebuilt trust and cultivated healthy relationships, breaking the cycle of fear and betrayal.

As our journey progressed, the book taught us to empower our inner child, encouraging us to reclaim our voices and redefine our identities. We set goals, embracing personal growth and resilience, no longer defined by the trauma of our past.

The book became our guide, leading us toward integration and healing. It illuminated a path towards forgiveness and let us release the burdens we carried for so long. Through its wisdom, we found the strength to heal, rewrite our stories, and create a brighter future.

Our lives transformed as we embraced the strategies within its pages. The book became more than words on paper—it became a catalyst for our healing, a testament to the resilience of the human spirit. From the depths of darkness, we emerged, nurtured by the power of self-discovery and armed with the tools to overcome our traumatic past.

And so, we stand today, survivors of a harrowing experience, united by the strength we found within ourselves and the guidance of *"Healing Complex PTSD."* Our story is one of hope and resilience, a testament to the transformative power of healing and the unwavering human spirit.

Welcome to *"Healing Complex PTSD,"* a book crafted with utmost care and compassion to guide you on a transformative journey toward healing and recovery. Within these pages, you will find a roadmap, a lifeline that offers solace, understanding, and practical strategies to help you navigate the complexities of your inner child's healing process.

This book is designed to assist those who have experienced the devastating impact of complex post-traumatic stress disorder (PTSD) in childhood. Whether you are a survivor of abuse, neglect, or other traumatic events, or if you are seeking to support a loved one on their healing journey, this book provides invaluable insights and actionable steps to facilitate healing, growth, and empowerment.

Through the seven practical strategies outlined in this book, you will embark on a path of self-discovery, self-compassion, and re-parenting. You will learn to reconnect with your inner child, foster a sense of safety and trust, heal traumatic memories, develop emotional regulation skills, rebuild relationships, empower your inner child, and integrate the past into a hopeful future.

Drawing upon evidence-based techniques, psychological insights, and real-life stories of resilience, "Healing Complex PTSD Child" serves as your companion, offering a sanctuary of understanding and support. It invites you to embark on a journey of self-exploration, guiding you through the healing process step by step.

No matter where you are in your healing journey, this book reminds you that you are not alone. It provides the tools, knowledge, and inspiration needed to transcend the pain of the past and embrace a brighter future. Together, let us walk this transformative path towards healing and recovery, nurturing the wounded inner child within us and reclaiming the joy, resilience, and strength that are rightfully ours.

Chapter One

Understanding Complex PTSD in Childhood: Unraveling the Hidden Impact of Trauma

Childhood should be a time of innocence, wonder, and exploration. Sadly, some children, teens and seniors had their early years marred by traumatic experiences that leave lasting scars. Complex Post-Traumatic Stress Disorder (PTSD) in children is a profound psychological condition that arises from prolonged exposure to trauma, often in the form of abuse, neglect, or chronic adversity. Understanding the complexities of this condition is crucial to providing effective support and healing for these young survivors.

Defining Complex PTSD in Childhood

Complex PTSD in children is an extension of the traditional PTSD diagnosis, encompassing a range of symptoms that arise from chronic or repeated trauma experienced during critical stages of development; unlike the more well-known PTSD, which stems from a single traumatic event, complex PTSD results from ongoing and pervasive trauma, often within the child's interpersonal relationships. This type of trauma disrupts the child's sense of safety, security, and trust in the world, leading to profound and long-lasting psychological effects.

The impact of complex PTSD on children is multifaceted and can permeate every aspect of their lives. Emotionally, these children may struggle with intense fear, shame, guilt, and confusion. They may exhibit difficulties regulating their emotions, leading to outbursts, withdrawal, or emotional numbing. Behaviorally, they may display aggression, defiance, self-harm, or engage in risky behaviors as maladaptive coping mechanisms. Cognitively, their ability to concentrate, learn, and retain information may be compromised. Physically, they may experience sleep disturbances, somatic complaints, and exhibit signs of hypervigilance or exaggerated startle responses.

Recognizing Symptoms and Signs

Recognizing the symptoms and signs of complex PTSD in children is essential for early identification and intervention. While each child's experience may manifest differently, common indicators include nightmares, flashbacks, intrusive thoughts, dissociation, anxiety, depression, avoidance of triggering situations, regression in developmental milestones, and difficulties with attachment and relationships. It is crucial to be attentive to these signs, as they serve as red flags signaling the need for support and intervention.

Unique Challenges Faced by Child Survivors

Child survivors of complex PTSD face unique challenges that necessitate a specialized approach to healing. Their developmental stage makes them more vulnerable to the impact of trauma, as their brains are still forming, and their coping mechanisms are limited. The trauma may disrupt their ability to form healthy attachments, trust others, and regulate their emotions effectively. Additionally, child survivors often internalize blame and shame, compounding the already complex healing process.

The Importance of Early Intervention and Support

Early intervention and support are paramount in addressing complex PTSD in children. Providing a safe and nurturing environment is crucial to re-establishing their sense of safety and trust. Access to trauma-informed therapies, such as play therapy, cognitive-behavioral therapy, and eye movement desensitization and reprocessing (EMDR), can help children process their trauma, develop coping skills, and build resilience. Equally important is the provision of social support networks, both within the family and in educational or community settings. These networks can offer validation, understanding, and stability, counteracting the isolation and emotional turmoil experienced by child survivors.

Chapter Two

Unveiling the Inner Child: Nurturing Healing and Reconnection

Within the depths of our beings lies an aspect of ourselves that holds the memories, emotions, and vulnerabilities of our childhood—the inner child. Chapter 2 of *"Healing Complex PTSD"* delves into the intricate world of the inner child, exploring the concept, understanding the impact of childhood trauma, recognizing its presence and needs, and providing guidance on nurturing and reconnecting with this wounded but resilient aspect of ourselves.

Discovering the Concept of the Inner Child

The concept of the inner child acknowledges that our childhood experiences shape our adult lives. It recognizes that the wounded and vulnerable child within us still longs for attention, validation, and healing. Our inner child holds our joys, our fears, and the pain we endured. By understanding and embracing this concept, we open the door to self-compassion, self-discovery, and the potential for profound healing.

Understanding the Impact of Childhood Trauma on the Inner Child

Childhood trauma leaves an indelible mark on our inner child. Whether it was abuse, neglect, or witnessing traumatic events, the impact is profound and enduring. The inner child carries the weight of these experiences, often manifesting in maladaptive coping mechanisms, relationship difficulties, and emotional turmoil. Recognizing the far-reaching impact of childhood trauma is essential in order to embark on the journey of healing and reclaiming our lives.

Recognizing the Presence and Needs of Your Inner Child

To embark on the path of healing, we must first recognize the presence of our inner child and acknowledge its needs. Through self-reflection and introspection, we become aware of the wounded aspects of ourselves that yearn for healing, validation, and love. It is through this recognition that we can offer the nurturing and compassionate support our inner child desperately seeks.

Nurturing and Reconnecting with Your Inner Child

Nurturing and reconnecting with our inner child is a delicate and transformative process. It requires creating a safe and loving space where our inner child can express itself freely. Engaging in self-care practices, such as journaling, meditation, and creative outlets, allows us to connect with our inner child and validate its emotions. By actively listening to our inner child's needs, we can provide the comfort and support it longs for, fostering a sense of safety and trust.

Drawing from our own experiences, we understand the significance of nurturing and reconnecting with our inner child. We have embarked on the journey ourselves, delving into the depths of our beings to uncover the wounds and fears that have held us captive. Through patience, self-compassion, and the guidance provided in "Healing Complex PTSD Child," we have learned to embrace our inner child, offering it the love and care it was denied in the past.

By nurturing and reconnecting with our inner child, we have experienced profound healing and transformation. The wounds of the past have begun to mend, and we have discovered a newfound sense of wholeness. Our inner child has become a source of strength, resilience, and creativity, reminding us of the beauty and joy that still resides within us.

Chapter Three

Building a Foundation of Safety and Trust

Chapter 3 of *"Healing Complex PTSD "* delves into the profound task of building a foundation of safety and trust. In this chapter, we explore practical strategies and actionable steps to create a safe environment for healing, establish trust in oneself and others, heal attachment wounds, and cultivate self-compassion and self-care practices.

Creating a Safe Environment for Healing

To create a safe environment for healing, it is crucial to establish physical and emotional safety. Physically, ensure that the surroundings are secure, comfortable, and free from any potential harm or triggers. Create a designated safe space—a peaceful sanctuary where the child can feel protected and at ease. Emotionally, foster an atmosphere of acceptance, empathy, and non-judgment. Communicate clearly and openly, validating the child's feelings and experiences. Encourage self-expression through art, journaling, or verbal communication, providing a safe outlet for emotions to be acknowledged and processed.

Establishing Trust in Oneself and Others

Rebuilding trust in oneself and others is a gradual process that requires patience and self-reflection. Begin by acknowledging and validating your own experiences, emotions, and strengths. Practice self-compassion and challenge self-doubt or negative self-talk. Engage in activities that promote self-esteem and personal growth. Surround yourself with supportive individuals who demonstrate consistency, respect, and empathy. Gradually open yourself to trusting others, starting with small steps and setting clear boundaries. As trust is developed, deepen relationships based on mutual understanding, reliability, and communication.

Healing Attachment Wounds and Building Healthy Relationships

Healing attachment wounds involves understanding and addressing the impacts of childhood trauma on relationships. Seek support from a therapist or counselor who specializes in attachment repair. Explore techniques such as schema therapy or eye movement desensitization and reprocessing (EMDR) to heal past attachment injuries. Practice open and honest communication, expressing needs and boundaries in relationships. Learn healthy relationship dynamics, including effective conflict resolution, active listening, and fostering emotional intimacy. Surround yourself with a supportive network of friends and loved ones who contribute positively to your healing journey.

Cultivating Self-Compassion and Self-Care Practices

Self-compassion is a vital component of healing. Self-compassion can be developed by treating yourself with kindness, understanding, and forgiveness. Use positive self-talk and confront self-critical thoughts. Engage in self-care practices that nurture your well-being, such as mindfulness, relaxation techniques, exercise, and hobbies that bring you joy. Prioritize self-care as an essential part of your routine, setting aside time for activities that replenish your physical, emotional, and mental reserves. Remember, self-compassion and self-care are not indulgences but essential practices for your healing and overall well-being.

Chapter Four

Strategy 1: Reconnecting With the Inner Child

Chapter 4 of *"Healing Complex PTSD "* delves into the transformative strategy of reconnecting with the inner child. Recognizing the importance of this connection, this chapter explores practical techniques to establish a deep bond and build trust with the wounded inner child. By focusing on rebuilding a sense of safety and security, child survivors of complex PTSD can embark on a profound journey of healing and growth.

Recognizing the Importance of Reconnecting with Your Inner Child

Reconnecting with the inner child is a pivotal step on the path of healing. The inner child represents the essence of who we were before the trauma and holds the wounds, emotions, and unmet needs from that time. By recognizing the importance of this connection, we acknowledge the vital role it plays in our healing journey. The inner child holds the keys to self-discovery, resilience, and the restoration of our authentic selves.

Practical Techniques to Establish a Connection and Build Trust

Establishing a connection with the inner child requires patience, empathy, and consistent effort. Here are practical techniques to facilitate this process:

1. **Inner Dialogue and Journaling:** Engage in inner dialogue by talking to your inner child. Start by expressing love, understanding, and compassion. Write letters to your inner child, acknowledging their pain and offering support and reassurance. Journaling allows for reflection and provides a safe space for the inner child's voice to be heard.

2. **Visualization and Guided Imagery:** Create a calming and safe visualization space in your mind where you can meet and interact with your inner child. Picture yourself in a serene setting and invite your inner child to join you. Engage in activities that bring joy and comfort to the inner child, such as playing, drawing, or talking.

3. **Creative Expression:** Utilize art, music, or other forms of creative expression as a means of connecting with your inner child. Engaging in artistic activities allows the inner child to communicate non-verbally, bypassing any barriers or resistance.

4. **Inner Child Meditation:** Practice meditation techniques that focus on the inner child. Visualize embracing and comforting your inner child, fostering a sense of safety, security, and acceptance. Repeat affirmations that reinforce love, worthiness, and healing.

Rebuilding a Sense of Safety and Security for Your Inner Child

Rebuilding a sense of safety and security for the inner child is crucial for healing. Here are actionable steps to foster a safe environment:

1. **Establish Boundaries:** Set clear boundaries to protect your inner child from further harm. Learn to say "no" to situations or people that trigger feelings of distress or

compromise your well-being. Prioritize self-care and ensure that your needs are met.

2. **Self-Soothing Techniques:** Develop self-soothing techniques that provide comfort and reassurance to your inner child. This can include deep breathing exercises, grounding techniques, or engaging in activities that promote relaxation, such as taking a bath or listening to calming music.

3. **Safety Rituals:** Create safety rituals that help your inner child feel secure. This can be as simple as establishing a consistent routine or creating a personal sanctuary where you can retreat when needed. Engaging in grounding exercises or using objects that bring a sense of comfort can also foster a feeling of safety.

4. **Inner Child Re-parenting:** Adopt a nurturing and loving role as the re-parenting figure for your inner child. Provide the care and validation they may have lacked during their traumatic experiences. Offer words of encouragement,

support, and compassion. Celebrate strengths and acknowledge resilience.

Reconnecting with the inner child is a solution-based strategy that facilitates healing and growth. By recognizing the importance of this connection, implementing practical techniques to establish a deep bond and trust, and rebuilding a sense of safety and security, child survivors of complex PTSD can embark on a transformative journey of self-discovery and healing.

Through personal experience, we understand the power of reconnecting with the inner child. We have embarked on this journey ourselves, facing the challenges and embracing the rewards. By employing these techniques, we have witnessed the profound transformation that can occur when we establish a loving and compassionate relationship with our inner child.

Chapter Five

Strategy 2: Healing Traumatic Memories - Liberating the Past for a Brighter Future

Chapter 5 of *"Healing Complex PTSD "* delves into Strategy 2: Healing Traumatic Memories. This chapter focuses on the vital task of releasing the grip of traumatic memories, allowing child survivors of complex PTSD to experience profound healing and pave the way for a brighter future. By understanding the mechanisms of how traumatic memories are stored and triggered, learning effective techniques to process and integrate these memories, and utilizing evidence-based therapeutic approaches, individuals can embark on a transformative journey of liberation and growth

Understanding How Traumatic Memories are Stored and Triggered

Traumatic memories are etched deeply within the psyche and body, stored differently from regular memories. They often encapsulate intense sensory details, emotions, and a sense of helplessness or danger. Understanding the mechanisms of how traumatic memories are stored and triggered is crucial in the healing process. These memories may be triggered by specific cues, such as sights, sounds, smells, or emotional states that resemble aspects of the original traumatic event. By becoming aware of these triggers, individuals can develop strategies to manage and cope with the reactivation of traumatic memories.

Processing and Integrating Traumatic Memories

Processing and integrating traumatic memories is a delicate and transformative endeavor. The following techniques can facilitate this process:

1. **Trauma-Focused Therapy:** Seek therapy from a trained professional who specializes in trauma-focused modalities. Approaches like Eye Movement Desensitization and Reprocessing (EMDR), Cognitive Processing Therapy (CPT), or Trauma-Focused Cognitive Behavioral Therapy (TF-CBT) offer structured frameworks for processing traumatic memories and promoting healing. These therapeutic approaches guide individuals through the

process of re-experiencing, reframing, and integrating traumatic memories, leading to their resolution.

2. **Narrative Therapy:** Engaging in narrative therapy can be immensely healing. By sharing your traumatic experiences in a safe and supportive environment, either through writing or verbal recounting, you can gain a sense of mastery and control over the narrative. This process allows you to examine the details of the traumatic event, explore its impact on your life, and reshape the meaning associated with the experience. This reframing helps facilitate integration and healing.

3. **Mindfulness-Based Techniques:** Mindfulness practices cultivate present-moment awareness and self-compassion, creating a safe container for processing traumatic memories. Mindfulness-based techniques, such as meditation, deep breathing exercises, or body scans, allow individuals to observe their thoughts and emotions without judgment or attachment. This practice can regulate emotional reactivity and create space for the processing and integration of traumatic memories.

Utilizing Evidence-Based Therapeutic Techniques for Trauma Resolution

Evidence-based therapeutic techniques provide valuable tools for trauma resolution. The following approaches have shown efficacy in promoting healing and integration:

1. **Eye Movement Desensitization and Reprocessing (EMDR):** EMDR utilizes bilateral stimulation, such as eye movements or tactile sensations, to facilitate the reprocessing of traumatic memories. By engaging in guided eye movements or other forms of bilateral stimulation, individuals desensitize the emotional charge associated with the memories. This process leads to their integration and resolution, fostering healing and a sense of closure.

2. **Cognitive Processing Therapy (CPT):** CPT focuses on challenging and restructuring maladaptive beliefs and thoughts associated with traumatic events. Through a systematic process, individuals examine the impact of trauma on their core beliefs and cognitions, identify distortions, and replace them with healthier perspectives.

This approach helps individuals gain a new understanding and develop a more balanced view of themselves and their experiences.

3. **Somatic Experiencing (SE):** Somatic Experiencing recognizes that trauma is held not only in the mind but also in the body. This approach focuses on releasing physical and emotional tension through gentle somatic techniques. By facilitating the renegotiation of traumatic experiences at a physiological level, individuals can discharge the trapped energy associated with the trauma, promoting healing and integration.

Emotional and Physical Trauma Release from the Body

Releasing emotional and physical trauma from the body is a vital aspect of the healing journey. The following practices can facilitate this release:

1. Body-Oriented Therapies: Engaging in body-oriented therapies, such as massage, acupuncture, yoga, or dance therapy, can help release stored tension and trauma from the body. These practices promote relaxation, grounding, and embodied healing. Through gentle movement, touch, and breath, individuals can access and release trauma held within their physical being.

2. Emotional Release Techniques: Emotional release techniques provide a safe space for expressing and processing intense emotions associated with traumatic memories. Engaging in expressive arts therapy, journaling, or talking with a trusted individual allows emotions to be witnessed and released. By honoring and acknowledging these emotions, individuals can gradually let go of the emotional charge attached to traumatic memories.

3. **Self-Care and Self-Compassion:** Prioritizing self-care practices that nourish the mind, body, and spirit is essential for the healing process. Engaging in activities that bring joy, relaxation, and comfort promotes overall well-being. Practicing self-compassion, offering understanding, kindness, and acceptance to oneself, allows for the integration of painful memories with self-love and forgiveness.

Healing traumatic memories is a solution-based strategy that liberates individuals from the weight of the past. By understanding how traumatic memories are stored and triggered, utilizing effective techniques to process and integrate these memories, and engaging in evidence-based therapeutic approaches, child survivors of complex PTSD can begin a transformative journey of healing, empowerment, and resilience.

Chapter Six

Strategy 3: Re-parenting the Inner Child - Nurturing the Wounded Self with Love and Compassion

In Chapter 6 of *"Healing Complex PTSD,"* we delve into the transformative strategy of re-parenting the inner child. This powerful approach involves becoming the loving and nurturing parent that our inner child needs to heal from the wounds of complex PTSD. By identifying and challenging negative beliefs and self-talk, applying re-parenting techniques to provide comfort, validation, and support, and fostering resilience and self-esteem in our inner child, we can offer the solutions necessary for profound healing and growth.

Becoming the Loving and Nurturing Parent Your Inner Child Needs

Re-parenting the inner child involves becoming the caring and nurturing parent we may have lacked during our childhood. By providing the love, care, and support that our inner child yearns for, we can create an environment conducive to healing and growth. Here are practical steps to become the loving and nurturing parent your inner child needs:

1. **Self-Reflection and Self-Compassion**: Engage in self-reflection to identify the areas where you may have lacked nurturing and support during your own childhood. Cultivate self-compassion by offering understanding, kindness, and forgiveness to yourself. Recognize that you have the power to break the cycle of neglect or abuse and provide a different experience for your inner child.

2. **Unconditional Love and Acceptance:** Offer your inner child unconditional love and acceptance. Embrace their vulnerabilities, fears, and pain with empathy and understanding. Practice self-love and extend that love to your inner child, reassuring them that they are worthy of love and deserving of happiness.

3. **Establish Healthy Boundaries:** Set healthy boundaries with others to protect your inner child. Advocate for your

needs and create a safe environment that nurtures your emotional and physical well-being. Boundaries help ensure that your inner child feels safe and secure.

Identifying and Challenging Negative Beliefs and Self-Talk

Negative beliefs and self-talk can hinder the healing process and perpetuate self-destructive patterns. To facilitate re-parenting, it is crucial to identify and challenge these negative narratives. Here's how to address negative beliefs and self-talk:

1. Self-Awareness and Mindfulness: Develop self-awareness of your thoughts and beliefs. Observe the negative self-talk patterns that arise and their impact on your emotions and behaviors. Practice mindfulness to cultivate a non-judgmental and compassionate attitude toward yourself.

2. Cognitive Restructuring: Challenge negative beliefs by examining the evidence supporting them. Replace distorted thoughts with more balanced and compassionate perspectives. Offer your inner child affirmations and positive statements that counteract the negative self-talk.

3. **Inner Dialogue and Positive Reinforcement:** Engage in an inner dialogue with your inner child. Offer words of encouragement, validation, and support. Provide positive reinforcement for your inner child's strengths, achievements, and efforts. Emphasize self-compassion and self-acceptance throughout the process.

Applying Re-parenting Techniques to Provide Comfort, Validation, and Support

Re-parenting techniques are essential for providing comfort, validation, and support to our inner child. These techniques can help repair past wounds and establish a secure and nurturing relationship within ourselves. Here are practical strategies to apply re-parenting techniques:

1. **Inner Child Dialogue:** Engage in dialogue with your inner child through writing or visualization exercises. Ask your inner child what they need and offer comfort, reassurance, and validation. Be present and attuned to their emotions, offering support and encouragement.

2. **Nurturing Activities:** Engage in activities that nourish and comfort your inner child. This may include engaging in creative pursuits, such as painting, writing, or playing an instrument. Engaging in playful activities, spending time in nature, or engaging in self-soothing rituals can also provide comfort and support.

3. **Comforting Inner Child Visualization:** Visualize holding your inner child in a comforting embrace. Imagine offering them warmth, protection, and love. Engage your senses to create a vivid experience of comfort and safety for your inner child.

Fostering Resilience and Self-Esteem in Your Inner Child

Building resilience and self-esteem is essential for the healing and growth of your inner child. Here are strategies to foster resilience and self-esteem:

1. **Recognize Strengths and Resilience:** Acknowledge and celebrate the strengths and resilience of your inner child. Reflect on past challenges they have overcome and emphasize their ability to overcome adversity. Affirm their strength and resilience in the face of trauma.

2. **Encourage Self-Care:** Prioritize self-care practices that nurture your inner child's well-being. Encourage activities that promote relaxation, joy, and self-expression. Cultivate self-compassion and self-acceptance, reinforcing the importance of taking care of oneself.

3. **Supportive Inner Voice:** Develop a supportive inner voice that encourages and uplifts your inner child. Replace self-critical thoughts with affirmations of self-worth, love, and encouragement. Offer reassurance during challenging

moments, reminding your inner child that they are capable and deserving of happiness.

Re-parenting the inner child is a solution-based strategy that allows us to provide the love, care, and support we may have missed during our childhood. By becoming the loving and nurturing parent our inner child needs, identifying and challenging negative beliefs and self-talk, applying re-parenting techniques to provide comfort, validation, and support, and fostering resilience and self-esteem, we offer powerful solutions for profound healing and growth.

Chapter Seven

Strategy 4: Emotional Regulation and Self-Soothing - Nurturing Inner Calm and Well-Being

In Chapter 7 of *"Healing Complex PTSD,"* we explore the transformative strategy of emotional regulation and self-soothing. This crucial aspect of healing empowers child survivors of complex PTSD to develop emotional regulation skills, learn effective coping mechanisms for emotional distress, practice mindfulness, and grounding techniques, and cultivate self-soothing strategies for their emotional well-being.

Developing Emotional Regulation Skills

Developing emotional regulation skills is essential for navigating the ups and downs of life. Here are practical solutions to develop emotional regulation skills:

1. **Emotional Awareness:** Cultivate emotional awareness by paying attention to your feelings and emotions in the present moment. Notice physical sensations associated with

different emotions, such as tension in the body or changes in breathing. This awareness allows you to identify and label your emotions, fostering self-understanding and regulation.

2. **Emotion Regulation Techniques:** Learn and practice emotion regulation techniques, such as deep breathing, progressive muscle relaxation, or guided imagery. These techniques can help you calm your nervous system, reduce emotional intensity, and restore balance during times of distress.

3. **Self-Reflection and Journaling:** Engage in self-reflection and journaling to explore and process your emotions. Write about your experiences, triggers, and emotional responses. This practice promotes self-awareness, insight, and the ability to regulate emotions effectively.

Learning Effective Coping Mechanisms for Emotional Distress

Learning effective coping mechanisms is crucial for managing emotional distress. Here are practical solutions to develop effective coping mechanisms:

1. **Healthy Coping Strategies:** Identify healthy coping strategies that work for you. This could include engaging in physical exercise, seeking support from loved ones, engaging in creative outlets like art or music, or practicing relaxation techniques such as meditation or deep breathing. Engaging in activities that bring joy and comfort can help alleviate emotional distress.

2. **Self-Compassion and Self-Care:** Cultivate self-compassion by offering yourself kindness and understanding during challenging emotional times. Prioritize self-care practices that nurture your well-being, such as engaging in hobbies, getting enough restful sleep, and maintaining a healthy lifestyle. These practices contribute to overall emotional resilience and well-being.

3. **Support Systems:** Build a support system of trusted individuals who can provide comfort and understanding during times of emotional distress. Reach out to friends, family, or therapists who can offer guidance, validation, and support. Connecting with others who can empathize and

provide a listening ear can help regulate emotions and provide a sense of comfort.

Practicing Mindfulness and Grounding Techniques

Mindfulness and grounding techniques help anchor us in the present moment and reduce emotional reactivity. Here are practical solutions to practice mindfulness and grounding:

1. **Mindful Awareness:** Cultivate a mindful awareness of the present moment. Pay nonjudgmental attention to your thoughts, feelings, and bodily sensations. This practice allows you to observe and acknowledge your emotions without getting caught up in their intensity, promoting emotional regulation.

2. **Grounding Exercises:** Engage in grounding exercises to bring your attention to the present moment and create a sense of stability. Focus on your senses by noticing the texture of an object, listening to the sounds around you, or feeling the sensation of your feet on the ground. Grounding techniques help redirect attention away from distressing emotions and foster a sense of calm and safety.

3. **Mindful Breathing:** Practice mindful breathing by focusing your attention on the sensation of your breath entering and leaving your body. Pay attention to the rhythm, depth, and quality of your breath. This simple yet powerful technique helps regulate emotions, reduces stress, and promotes relaxation.

Cultivating Self-Soothing Strategies for Emotional Well-Being

Self-soothing strategies play a vital role in nurturing emotional well-being. Here are practical solutions to cultivate self-soothing strategies:

1. **Sensory Soothing:** Engage in sensory soothing activities that provide comfort and relaxation. This can include taking a warm bath, cuddling up with a soft blanket, listening to soothing music, or engaging in aromatherapy. Engaging your senses in soothing experiences helps calm the nervous system and promote emotional well-being.

2. **Self-Comforting Gestures:** Develop self-comforting gestures that elicit a sense of safety and care. This can include hugging yourself, placing a hand on your heart, or engaging in gentle self-massage. These gestures send signals of comfort and compassion to your inner child, promoting self-soothing and emotional regulation.

3. **Positive Affirmations:** Practice positive affirmations that nurture self-compassion and self-esteem. Repeat affirmations such as "I am safe and loved," "I am capable of handling my emotions," or "I am deserving of happiness and peace." These affirmations counter negative self-talk and cultivate a sense of self-worth and emotional well-being.

Emotional regulation and self-soothing provide powerful solutions for child survivors of complex PTSD to navigate their emotional landscape with resilience and well-being. By developing emotional regulation skills, learning effective coping mechanisms, practicing mindfulness and grounding techniques, and cultivating self-soothing strategies, individuals can nurture inner calm, find emotional balance, and experience profound healing.

Chapter Eight

Strategy 5: Rebuilding Trust and Relationships - Nurturing Connections for Healing and Growth

Chapter 8 of *"Healing Complex PTSD"* delves into Strategy 5: Rebuilding Trust and Relationships. This chapter explores the profound impact of trauma on trust, the process of rebuilding trust in oneself and others, nurturing healthy and supportive relationships, and establishing boundaries and communication skills.

Understanding the Impact of Trauma on Trust

Trauma can profoundly impact an individual's ability to trust. Experiences of betrayal, abuse, and neglect can shatter one's sense of safety and make it challenging to trust oneself and others. Understanding the impact of trauma on trust is essential for healing. Here are practical solutions to navigate this process:

1. **Acknowledge the Impact:** Recognize and validate the impact trauma has had on your ability to trust. Understand

that it is a natural response to traumatic experiences. Validate your own feelings and experiences without judgment, allowing yourself to process and heal at your own pace.

2. **Trauma-Informed Therapy:** Engage in trauma-informed therapy with a qualified professional who can provide a safe and supportive environment. Trauma-focused therapies, such as EMDR or Trauma-Focused Cognitive Behavioral Therapy (TF-CBT), can help address the underlying wounds that affect trust and provide tools for healing and rebuilding trust.

3. **Self-Compassion:** Cultivate self-compassion as you navigate the journey of rebuilding trust. Offer understanding, kindness, and patience to yourself. Recognize that trust takes time and that healing is a gradual process. Practice self-care and self-soothing techniques to support yourself along the way.

Rebuilding Trust in Oneself and Others

Rebuilding trust is an essential part of the healing process. Here are practical solutions to rebuild trust in oneself and others:

1. **Building Self-Trust:** Start by rebuilding trust in yourself. Honor your commitments to yourself, set realistic goals, and follow through with self-care practices. Celebrate your accomplishments, no matter how small. As you consistently show up for yourself, trust in your ability to make choices that serve your well-being will naturally grow.

2. **Honoring Boundaries:** Establish and honor personal boundaries to protect your physical and emotional well-being. Communicate your boundaries clearly and assertively, and expect them to be respected. This practice builds self-trust and reinforces the belief that you have the right to be safe and respected in all relationships.

3. **Seeking Support:** Surround yourself with supportive individuals who demonstrate trustworthiness. Seek out relationships with people who are compassionate, understanding, and trustworthy. Engage in therapy, support

groups, or trusted friendships to build connections with those who can provide a safe space for healing and growth.

Nurturing Healthy and Supportive Relationships

Nurturing healthy and supportive relationships is essential for healing from complex PTSD. Here are practical solutions to cultivate meaningful connections:

1. **Open Communication:** Foster open and honest communication in your relationships. Share your needs, fears, and boundaries with trusted individuals. Practice active listening and offer understanding and empathy to others. Effective communication creates a foundation of trust and promotes healthy relationships.

2. **Emotional Support:** Seek and offer emotional support within your relationships. Create a safe space for vulnerability, allowing yourself and others to express emotions without judgment. Show empathy and validation, knowing that support is essential for healing and growth.

3. **Mutual Respect:** Cultivate relationships based on mutual respect. Expect others to treat you with kindness, compassion, and understanding. Respect each other's boundaries, opinions, and individuality. Healthy relationships are built on a foundation of trust and respect.

Establishing Boundaries and Communication Skills

Establishing boundaries and developing effective communication skills are vital components of rebuilding trust and nurturing healthy relationships. Here are practical solutions to establish boundaries and enhance communication:

1. **Boundary Setting:** Clearly define your boundaries and communicate them assertively and respectfully. Practice saying "no" when needed and prioritize your own well-being. Be consistent in upholding your boundaries and expect them to be respected by others.

2. **Active Listening:** Cultivate active listening skills to foster effective communication. Give your full attention to the speaker, maintain eye contact, and offer nonverbal cues that

show you are engaged. Reflect back on what the speaker has shared to ensure understanding and validate their experiences.

3. **Conflict Resolution:** Learn and practice healthy conflict resolution skills. Approach conflicts with empathy and a willingness to understand the other person's perspective. Use "I" statements to express your feelings and needs without blaming or attacking them. Seek solutions that are mutually beneficial and promote understanding and compromise.

Rebuilding trust and relationships is a solution-based strategy that empowers individuals to heal from the wounds of complex PTSD. By understanding the impact of trauma on trust, rebuilding trust in oneself and others, nurturing healthy and supportive relationships, and establishing boundaries and communication skills, child survivors of complex PTSD can cultivate meaningful connections and experience profound healing and growth.

Chapter Nine

Strategy 6: Empowering the Inner Child - Unleashing Strength, Growth, and Resilience

In Chapter 9 of *"Healing Complex PTSD "* we explore the transformative strategy of empowering the inner child. This chapter focuses on encouraging empowerment and self-advocacy, cultivating strengths and talents, setting goals and embracing personal growth, and fostering resilience and embracing positive change.

Encouraging Empowerment and Self-Advocacy

Encouraging empowerment and self-advocacy is crucial for the healing and growth of the inner child. Here are practical solutions to foster empowerment and self-advocacy:

1. Self-Reflection: Engage in self-reflection to identify your values, strengths, and areas for growth. Understand your preferences, needs, and boundaries. This self-awareness forms the foundation for empowerment and self-advocacy.

2. **Assertiveness Training:** Learn and practice assertiveness skills to effectively communicate your needs, boundaries, and opinions. Develop the ability to express yourself confidently and assertively while respecting the rights and boundaries of others. Assertiveness empowers the inner child to stand up for themselves and navigate relationships with confidence.

3. **Self-Empowering Beliefs:** Cultivate self-empowering beliefs that reinforce your worth and potential. Challenge self-limiting beliefs and replace them with positive and affirming thoughts. Develop a growth mindset that embraces challenges as opportunities for learning and personal development.

Cultivating Strengths and Talents

Cultivating strengths and talents nurtures the inner child's sense of self-worth and identity. Here are practical solutions to cultivate strengths and talents:

1. **Self-Discovery:** Engage in self-discovery to identify your unique strengths and talents. Reflect on activities that bring you joy and fulfillment. Explore different interests and passions to uncover hidden talents. Embracing and developing these strengths fosters a sense of empowerment and confidence.

2. **Skill Development:** Invest time and effort in developing your identified strengths and talents. Enroll in classes, workshops, or training programs to enhance your skills. Seek opportunities to apply and showcase your abilities, allowing your inner child to shine and grow.

3. **Celebrating Accomplishments:** Celebrate your accomplishments, no matter how small. Acknowledge and appreciate the progress you make in developing your strengths and talents. This positive reinforcement fuels motivation and confidence, empowering the inner child to continue their journey of growth.

Setting Goals and Embracing Personal Growth

Setting goals and embracing personal growth is essential for the inner child's development and healing. Here are practical solutions to set goals and embrace personal growth:

1. **Goal-Setting:** Set specific, realistic, and meaningful goals that align with your values and aspirations. Break larger goals into smaller, manageable steps to facilitate progress. Write down your goals and track your progress to stay motivated and focused.

2. **Personal Development Activities:** Engage in personal development activities, such as reading self-help books, attending workshops, or participating in therapy or coaching. These activities provide tools and insights for personal growth, fostering resilience and self-discovery.

3. **Embracing Challenges:** Embrace challenges as opportunities for growth. Take calculated risks and step outside of your comfort zone. Embracing challenges builds resilience, confidence, and the ability to navigate adversity effectively.

Fostering Resilience and Embracing Positive Change

Fostering resilience and embracing positive change is essential for the inner child's healing journey. Here are practical solutions to foster resilience and embrace positive change:

1. **Self-Care Practices:** Prioritize self-care practices that nourish your physical, emotional, and mental well-being. Participate in activities that promote relaxation, mindfulness, and introspection. Self-care strengthens resilience and equips the inner child to navigate life's challenges.

2. **Building Support Networks:** Cultivate a support network of trusted individuals who uplift and encourage you. Surround yourself with people who believe in your potential and offer support during difficult times. Seek out communities, therapy groups, or support groups that foster connection and provide a safe space for growth.

3. **Embracing Flexibility:** Embrace flexibility and adaptability in the face of change. Recognize that change is a normal part of life and that it can bring about new opportunities and growth. Develop problem-solving skills and a positive mindset that embraces change as a catalyst for personal transformation.

Empowering the inner child is a solution-based strategy that unlocks their strength, growth, and resilience. By encouraging empowerment and self-advocacy, cultivating strengths and talents, setting goals and embracing personal growth, and fostering resilience and embracing positive change, child survivors of complex PTSD can begin a transformative journey of self-discovery and empowerment.

Chapter Ten

Strategy 7: Integration and Continued Healing - Embracing Wholeness and Celebrating Growth

In Chapter 10 of *"Healing Complex PTSD,"* we explore the transformative strategy of integration and continued healing. This chapter focuses on integrating the healed aspects of the inner child with the present self, embracing forgiveness and letting go of the past, sustaining long-term recovery and growth, and celebrating the resilience and growth of your inner child.

Integrating the Healed Aspects of the Inner Child with the Present Self

Integrating the healed aspects of the inner child with the present self is a powerful process that fosters wholeness and alignment. Here are practical solutions to facilitate integration:

1. **Inner Child Dialogue:** Engage in regular inner child dialogue to deepen the connection with your healed inner

child. Communicate with them, listen to their needs, and integrate their wisdom and strengths into your present self. Embrace the lessons and resilience they offer.

2. **Embracing Vulnerability:** Allow yourself to be vulnerable and open to emotions that arise from integrating the healed aspects of your inner child. Embrace the full range of emotions and honor the healing process as you merge the past and present selves. Trust in your ability to navigate this integration with compassion and self-acceptance.

3. **Embodying Healing Practices:** Practice embodiment techniques, such as yoga, dance, or mindful movement, to connect with the physical sensations and emotions associated with the integration process. Embodying the healing practices allows you to experience the integration at a deeper level, fostering a sense of wholeness and alignment.

Forgiving and Letting Go of the Past

Embracing forgiveness and letting go of the past is essential for the inner child's healing journey. Here are practical solutions to facilitate forgiveness and release:

1. **Self-Forgiveness:** Offer forgiveness to yourself for any perceived shortcomings or regrets from the past. Recognize that you did the best you could with the resources you had at the time. Practice self-compassion and let go of self-blame and shame. Embrace the journey of self-forgiveness as an act of liberation and self-love.

2. **Compassion for Others:** Cultivate compassion for those who may have caused harm or pain during your childhood. Recognize that they, too, may have been wounded and acting from their own unhealed experiences. Practice empathy and release any resentment or anger that may be holding you back.

3. **Letting Go Rituals:** Engage in letting go rituals to symbolize the release of the past. This could include writing a letter to the past, burning it, or creating a symbolic

representation of letting go. These rituals provide closure and support the process of forgiveness and moving forward.

Sustaining Long-Term Recovery and Growth

Sustaining long-term recovery and growth is a lifelong journey. Here are practical solutions to support ongoing healing and growth:

1. **Self-Care as a Priority:** Prioritize self-care practices as a foundation for sustained recovery and growth. Take part in activities that will benefit your physical, emotional, and spiritual well-being. Practice self-compassion and make self-care a non-negotiable aspect of your daily life.

2. **Ongoing Therapy and Support:** Continue engaging in therapy or counseling to support your healing journey. Regularly check in with a qualified professional who can provide guidance, insights, and tools to navigate challenges and sustain long-term growth. Seek support from trusted individuals who understand your journey.

3. **Mindfulness and Reflection**: Cultivate mindfulness practices and regular self-reflection to stay connected to your inner self. Make time for reflection, meditation, or journaling. These practices foster self-awareness, self-discovery, and ongoing healing.

Celebrating the Resilience and Growth of Your Inner Child

Celebrating the resilience and growth of your inner child is a powerful way to honor the progress made on your healing journey. Here are practical solutions to celebrate:

1. **Gratitude Practice:** Practice gratitude by acknowledging and appreciating the progress you have made. Reflect on the resilience and growth of your inner child. Embrace a mindset of gratitude for the lessons learned and the strength gained through your healing process.

2. **Milestone Celebrations:** Celebrate significant milestones and achievements along your healing journey. Recognize the courage and determination it took to reach these milestones.

Treat yourself with kindness and celebrate the resilience and growth of your inner child.

3. **Expressing Authenticity:** Embrace your authentic self and express it freely. Celebrate your unique qualities, interests, and strengths. Engage in activities that bring you joy and allow your inner child to shine. Embracing authenticity fosters a sense of empowerment and celebrates the journey of self-discovery.

Integration and continued healing is a solution-based strategy that allows the inner child to experience wholeness and celebrate ongoing growth. By integrating the healed aspects of the inner child with the present self, embracing forgiveness and letting go of the past, sustaining long-term recovery and growth, and celebrating the resilience and growth of your inner child, child survivors of complex PTSD can embark on a transformative journey of self-empowerment and fulfillment.

Bonus

Self-Assessment Exercises

Within the pages of *"Healing Complex PTSD,"* we provide a powerful bonus: a collection of self-assessment exercises designed to deepen self-awareness, foster healing, and promote personal growth. These exercises offer you an opportunity to reflect, evaluate, and gain insights into your journey of complex PTSD recovery. By engaging in these exercises, you can cultivate a deeper understanding of your triggers, emotions, boundaries, resilience, and overall well-being. Through self-reflection and exploration, you can pave the way for transformation and empower yourself on your healing path.

1. Create a list of situations, people, or experiences that trigger intense emotional or physical reactions. Rate the intensity of each trigger on a scale of 1-10 and identify coping strategies that have been helpful in managing these triggers.

2. Take a moment to tune into your emotions. Rate your current emotional state on a scale of 1-10 for various emotions such as anger, sadness, fear, and joy. Reflect on any patterns or triggers that contribute to these emotions and brainstorm healthy coping strategies.

3. Reflect on how you treat yourself during challenging times. Are you self-critical or self-compassionate? Write down instances where you can practice self-compassion and explore ways to be kinder and more nurturing to yourself.

4. Assess your personal boundaries in different areas of your life, such as relationships, work, and self-care. Identify any areas where your boundaries might be too rigid or too loose, and brainstorm strategies for setting and maintaining healthy boundaries.

5. Reflect on past experiences where you have shown resilience and overcome adversity. Write down the skills, strengths, and resources you utilized during those times. Identify how you can apply those same qualities to your current healing journey.

_____
_____
_____
_____
_____
_____
_____
_____
_____
_____
_____
_____
_____
_____
_____
_____

6. Make a list of coping strategies you currently use to manage stress and triggers. Evaluate their effectiveness and identify any strategies that might be helpful to incorporate into your self-care routine.

7. Evaluate the strength and availability of your support system. Identify individuals who provide understanding, validation, and encouragement. Reflect on whether there are any gaps in your support network and explore ways to seek additional support if needed.

8. Reflect on your sense of self-worth and self-esteem. Identify any negative beliefs or internalized messages that impact your self-worth. Challenge these beliefs and replace them with positive, affirming statements.

9. Assess how trauma has affected various aspects of your daily life, such as relationships, work, and self-care. Identify areas where you may need additional support or tools to manage the impact of trauma and make a plan to address those areas.

10. Take a moment to reflect on your personal growth and healing journey. Write down the progress you have made, the challenges you have overcome, and the areas you still wish to work on. Acknowledge and celebrate the steps you have taken toward healing.

These self-assessment exercises are designed to promote self-reflection, awareness, and growth. They can help individuals with Complex PTSD gain insights into their experiences and identify areas for personal development and healing.

Bonus Two

Positive Affirmations

These positive affirmations are meant to uplift, inspire, and reinforce a positive mindset for PTSD warriors. Repeat them regularly, embrace their empowering messages, and let them guide you on your path to healing and reclaiming your life.

1. I am strong, resilient, and capable of healing from my past traumas.

2. I deserve love, compassion, and understanding as I navigate my healing journey.

3. I am not defined by my past experiences. I am creating a new and empowered future.

4. I am safe in the present moment, and I trust that I have the strength to overcome any challenges that arise.

5. I am deserving of self-care and prioritizing my own well-being. My healing is a priority.

6. I release the weight of guilt and blame. I forgive myself for any perceived shortcomings and embrace self-compassion.

7. I am not alone in my journey. I have a support network that understands and believes in my healing process.

8. Each day, I am taking steps toward healing, growth, and reclaiming my inner power.

9. I choose to let go of negative thoughts and beliefs that no longer serve me. I embrace positivity and self-empowerment.

10. I am resilient, and my past traumas do not define me. I am creating a life filled with joy, purpose, and fulfillment.

Conclusion

In *"Healing Complex PTSD,"* we have embarked on a transformative journey of healing, growth, and empowerment for child survivors of complex post-traumatic stress disorder. This book has been crafted with deep empathy, personal experiences, and a solution-based approach to provide valuable insights, practical strategies, and profound support.

Throughout its pages, we have explored the multifaceted aspects of complex PTSD, from understanding its definition and impact on children to recognizing the signs and symptoms. We have delved into the importance of reconnecting with the inner child, building a foundation of safety and trust, healing traumatic memories, and embracing the transformative power of re-parenting the inner child.

We have navigated the realms of emotional regulation and self-soothing, rebuilding trust and relationships, empowering the inner child, and cultivating resilience. Our focus has been on integrating healing, embracing forgiveness, sustaining long-term recovery and growth, and celebrating the journey of the inner child.

As we conclude this book, we want to remind you that you are not alone in your healing journey. Your experiences are valid, and your path to recovery is unique. By implementing the strategies, exercises, and affirmations presented, you have the power to reclaim your life, rewrite your story, and embark on a future defined by strength, resilience, and inner peace.

May this book serve as a guiding light, providing solace, validation, and practical tools to support your healing process. Remember, healing is a gradual process, and self-compassion is key. You have the strength within you to overcome the challenges, nurture your inner child, and to create a life filled with joy, purpose, and fulfillment.

You are a survivor, a warrior, and an inspiration. Embrace your journey, celebrate your growth, and know that you have the power to heal and thrive. You are deserving of love, compassion, and a life that is free from the shackles of the past. Trust in yourself, embrace the power of healing, and step into a future where your inner child can flourish and soar.

This is your story of healing, and we are honored to have played a part in your journey. May you find the peace, strength, and resilience you seek, and may your inner child find solace, love, and a renewed sense of wonder.

Appreciation

Dear Reader,

We want to express our heartfelt gratitude for choosing **"Healing Complex PTSD"** as your guide on the path to healing and transformation. Your decision to embark on this journey with us signifies your courage and determination to overcome the challenges of complex post-traumatic stress disorder (PTSD).

We understand that healing can be a challenging and deeply personal process. That's why we want you to know that we are here for you every step of the way. If you encounter any difficulties while using this book, please reach out to us at wintonconsults@gmail.com and we promise to respond within 24 hours with support and guidance.

Your feedback is invaluable to us. We would be immensely grateful if you could take a moment to leave a positive review about "Healing Complex PTSD" in the website. Your review will not only serve as a token of appreciation for our work but also provide encouragement to others who may be seeking solace and healing.

Remember, you are not alone in your struggles. We stand with you, offering our unwavering support and commitment to your healing journey. Together, let us pave the way to a future defined by strength, resilience, and inner peace.

With heartfelt thanks,

Dr. Kaden Winton and the Healing Complex PTSD Team

Picture Links

https://images.pexels.com/photos/3554374/pexels-photo-3554374.jpeg?auto=compress&cs=tinysrgb&w=600

https://images.pexels.com/photos/7224077/pexels-photo-7224077.jpeg?auto=compress&cs=tinysrgb&w=600&lazy=load

https://images.pexels.com/photos/3958462/pexels-photo-3958462.jpeg?auto=compress&cs=tinysrgb&w=600&lazy=load

https://images.pexels.com/photos/8533232/pexels-photo-8533232.jpeg?auto=compress&cs=tinysrgb&w=600&lazy=load

https://images.pexels.com/photos/4116674/pexels-photo-4116674.jpeg?auto=compress&cs=tinysrgb&w=600&lazy=load

https://images.pexels.com/photos/5970111/pexels-photo-5970111.jpeg?auto=compress&cs=tinysrgb&w=600&lazy=load

Milton Keynes UK
Ingram Content Group UK Ltd.
UKHW020738180224
437973UK00014B/1571